In… ng facts for ROBLOX FANS

Unofficial collection

Luprion

Our promise

Should there be any issue with the order,
if the product arrives damaged, or you are not satisfied with the product, then please contact us within 30 days of ordering and we will refund your purchase.

We are 100% committed to our products and will strive to ensure your complete satisfaction with the product.

Expectations fulfilled?

Are you satisfied with the product?
Then we would be delighted if you would let us know what you think by leaving a review on Amazon. Even a single sentence makes a big difference.
This way you can help other customers with their purchase decision.
We also look forward to your personal message. Simply write to us at:

kontakt@luprion.com

Contents of this book

We regularly check the contents of this book to ensure that they are up to date. Nevertheless, incorrect information can sometimes slip in. If you notice something like this, please let us know using the email adress adove.

Foreword

Anyone who has ever immersed themselves in the world of Roblox knows how versatile and exciting this game can be. There is so much to discover, build, and experience. But sometimes it's good to take a little break and do something else—something that isn't necessarily necessary for success in the game, but can still be entertaining and interesting.

That's exactly why we wrote this book. It's a collection of entertaining and surprising facts about Roblox – perhaps not crucial to the game, but amusing, exciting, and sometimes even astonishing.

Think of it as a little break from everyday life in Roblox, an opportunity to see the game from a new perspective and maybe even expand your knowledge. Because even the seemingly useless can have its own charm and bring joy.

This book does not claim to be a guide or manual for Roblox. Rather, it is an invitation to sit back, relax, and explore the world of Roblox in a casual, lighthearted way.

We hope you enjoy reading this book as much as we enjoyed writing it. Immerse yourself in the world of curious Roblox facts and prepare to be surprised!

From simulation to sensation

Before Roblox achieved its current popularity, it benefited greatly from the expertise of a company called "Knowledge Revolution", which specialized in the development of physics simulation software. Many of the early employees, including top graduates and experienced developers, were recruited from this talented pool. Although the gaming platform did not yet have a big name in its early days, it was Knowledge Revolution's excellent reputation that made it possible to assemble a strong, knowledgeable team and bring the game to life.

From children's picture to horror hit

If you're a fan of horror games, you've probably heard of a certain survival game where you have to flee from an evil, animal-like creature. But what you may not know is that this Roblox experience, known as "Piggy," had a surprisingly harmless inspiration. Originally, the idea for the game was just a simple 2D image of Peppa Pig chasing through a house. It was only after this simple concept that the game evolved into what we know today: a complex survival horror game where players collect tools and keys to escape the evil, animal-like creature.

The in-game name of David Baszucki, co-founder and CEO of Roblox Corporation, is "builderman."

Short and Sweet

The acid block in the Piggy experience is a unique element in build mode, as it is the only block with a glowing color. Touching it will cause damage, giving Piggy a strategic advantage. Piggy can use these blocks to trap you in certain areas or corner you to make you easier to catch.

♡

In RIVALS, there are two skins that stand out due to a special feature: Karambit and Candy Cane. When these skins are equipped, no sound is emitted, unlike most other skins. It is currently unclear whether this is an intentional feature by the developers or an unintended effect.

♡

Currently, “The Mines” in DOORS poses the most danger of all levels.

♡

When you hold the Cursed Dual Katana in Blox Fruits, you move slightly faster than normal, almost imperceptibly.

Short and Sweet

In the Roblox experience "DOORS," it is implied that the player has died many times but always returned. This assumption is reinforced by dialogues between Curious Light and Guiding Light. The game mechanics, which seem to be closely linked to Guiding Light, also support this interpretation.

♡

The "Pizza Planet" pizzeria in the "Welcome to Bloxburg" experience is a direct reference to the fictional restaurant of the same name from the animated film "Toy Story."

♡

The Nihonzaru from Grow a Garden is another name for the Japanese macaque, a species of monkey that actually exists.

From gibberish to tragedy

In the fifth chapter of Piggy: Book 1, entitled "School," the canonical bot is the teacher. One of the classrooms holds a secret that has been immortalized on a blackboard. At first glance, the message there seems like gibberish: "Z wvvc vmvipkyzex Z uf. Z tre'k tfekifc dp rtkzfej. Z tre'k yvcg dpjvcw. Dp dzeu pvccj wfi yvcg slk dp sfup ufvj efk rxivv. Z nzjy kyv nficu nflcu leuvijkreu."

Most players pay no further attention to this cryptic text and ignore it. But when the characters are correctly deciphered, a profound and tragic message is revealed. It reads: "I feel everything I do. I can't control my actions. I can't help myself. My mind is screaming for help, but my body won't let it. I wish the world would understand."

It is believed that these words were written by the teacher before she became fully infected. They provide a harrowing insight into her desperate inner struggle and explain why she became the bot character feared by players.

Hunting badges à la influencer

Imagine you're playing your favorite game and suddenly a unique badge appears on your profile. What if it wasn't awarded for reaching a certain level or defeating a boss, but simply for being in the right place at the right time? In Royale High, players can earn special "influencer badges." However, these awards are not given out by an algorithm, but directly by famous content creators who happen to be playing on the same server. It's important to note, though, that it's entirely up to the individual YouTuber or influencer whether this feature is enabled at all.

Winter duel between like-minded players

In the update on December 21, 2024, snowballs were introduced as throwable objects in The Strongest Battlegrounds. Their special feature was that they only affected players who were also using snowballs. This mechanic was probably designed to encourage players to participate in large snowball fights and get quick, easy kills. At the same time, this rule ensured that players who did not want to participate were not disturbed by them.

Roblox is particularly popular with children: around 40% of players are aged 12 or younger, and 20% are even under 9. Only around 19% are aged 25 or older. The majority are boys, and 8 out of 10 play on a mobile phone or tablet.

Weather madness in the garden

Just as we often plan our days around the weather forecast in the real world, the cycles of nature are also important in the virtual world, especially in an experience like "Grow a Garden" on Roblox. Players looking for patterns to optimize their harvests have discovered fascinating facts about the frequency of various weather phenomena, even though these have never been officially confirmed by the developers. Rain is the most frequent visitor to the game world, providing a shower about every 20 minutes. Thunderstorms are much rarer, occurring only every 2 to 6 hours and bringing a special atmosphere. The rarest and most impressive phenomenon is a meteor shower, which lights up the night sky only once every few nights. The frost weather type was originally removed from the game during the "Summer Harvest Event," but is now available again.

John Doe attacks

In March 2017, a wild rumor circulated: the mysterious account JohnDoe would hack the entire Roblox platform on March 18. YouTube was flooded with dramatic videos, alleged threat messages, and conspiracy theories. But Roblox soon clarified that JohnDoe was just an old test account and posed no threat. Nevertheless, new "hacker" legends such as TheC0mmunity and BloxWatch soon followed, who also wanted to "destroy" Roblox. Spoiler: These were all jokes too. Not a single hack, just a lot of drama.

More sections than days in a year

Think you know every nook and cranny of Tower of Hell? Then take a guess: how many different sections are there in this gigantic tower? You might be surprised, because there are far more than you think. Currently (as of July 2025), there are no fewer than 470 sections in Tower of Hell. This impressive total is divided into 330 vanilla sections, 35 removed sections, 32 secret sections (2 are event-specific and now inaccessible, 5 require admin commands to spawn), 51 moded sections (removed), 14 horizontal sections, 1 finish section with 4 additional RB variants, 3 start sections (1 made inaccessible).

When reality comes into play

On the "Hospital 3" map in Murder Mystery 2, there is an interesting discovery to be made outside the hospital: you can see a man on a stretcher wearing a "Thrasher" shirt and with a broken leg. A nurse with a skateboard is accompanying him. This scene is a reference to a real event: YouTuber and map developer "Thexz" (also known as 'Joven'), who creates maps for "Nikilis," actually broke his leg.

The colorful world of BedWars maps

BedWars offers a wide selection of maps that span all game modes. Each map has a unique design, atmosphere, and concept. Some maps, such as Forest, Blossom, and Glacier, were reworked shortly after their release because there were too many places where players could fall. For example, the original Blossom map had two floors.

The Western and Volcano maps were the first to be added for both Duo and Squad modes. The Volcano and Farm maps are unique in that they have five emerald generators, while most others only have four. Many newer maps have five generators in Solo and Doubles modes, but not in Squads mode. The 16v16 and 30v30 game modes use the same maps. Solo and Doubles modes also share most maps, but not all maps can be played in both modes.

The map "Savannah" is probably the most mysterious, as virtually nothing is known about it except its release date. There are two separate maps called Castle: one for 16v16 mode and another for Skull Drop mode. The Treehouse map originally had zip lines, but these have since been removed.

Confusingly similar

Many players believe that the victory melodies in Murder Mystery 2 are taken from well-known songs – such as "Imagine" for the murderer or "I Respect You" for the hero. But that's a mistake! In fact, both melodies were composed in the music app GarageBand. The killer's victory sound uses the "Zippy Synth" in combination with the "Clock Sync Beat 0," while the hero's victory was created with the "Above and Beyond Synth" and the "Almost Electro Beat."

Déjà vu on eight legs

Sometimes in everyday life, you encounter a movement, a style, or a sound that seems unmistakably familiar—a kind of déjà vu. This is also the case for gamers who find themselves in completely different worlds and yet encounter similar animations. This feeling of recognition is no coincidence in the Roblox experience "The Strongest Battlegrounds," especially when facing the boss crab. The impressive and intimidating animations of this enemy, who swings his massive claws and stomps across the battlefield, are largely taken directly from the enormous crabs and giant lobsters in the games "Dark Souls 3" and "Elden Ring." Only the breathtaking attacks "Giant Leap" and "Laser Claws" have been added as unique additions, making the boss crab a small but significant cultural crossover in the world of video games.

Short and Sweet

There are approximately 5.8 billion registered accounts on Roblox.

The subway in Roblox Brookhaven is the only automated rail transport system you will find there.

Originally, the colors of the sections in Tower of Hell were supposed to reflect their difficulty.

There are currently 16 antique weapons in Murder Mystery 2 (as of July 2025).

Bamboo seeds are among the most common legendary seeds that can be purchased in Sam's shop. When restocking, it is possible to find up to 20 of these seeds.

Short and Sweet

David Baszucki's parents are from Ukraine.

♡

If the sheriff leaves the game during a round in Murder Mystery 2, his weapon disappears—and with it, the only chance to stop the murderer. This gives the murderer a clear advantage.

♡

The "8-Bit Item Pack" in Murder Mystery 2 has been purchased by 1,131 players.

♡

Users reacted to the announcement of the Tix abolition with skepticism. Since it occurred two weeks before April 1st, some suspected it was an April Fool's joke.

♡

Rotten Robbie, the gas station in Brookhaven, is named after a real American gas station chain.

In October 2021, Roblox entered into a partnership with Chipotle Mexican Grill, a well-known US fast food chain famous for its Mexican dishes such as burritos and tacos. As part of the "Halloween Burrito" promotion, Chipotle gave away burritos worth a total of $1 million every day to the first 30,000 participants.

Short and Sweet

In the eighth chapter of Piggy: Book 2, which is the 20th chapter of the series overall, you board the ship. This chapter is particularly significant for the creator of the experience, MiniToon, as it is his personal favorite in Book 2.

♡

When a Roblox game goes viral on TikTok, it often has a direct impact on Twitch. Games such as "Steal a Brainrot" and "DOORS" experienced sudden spikes in viewership because curious fans wanted to see live reactions.

♡

The YouTube video "GIANT vs TINY – Roblox Obby" was published three years ago and now has over 143 million views, making it the most clicked Roblox video on YouTube!

♡

Brookhaven RP currently hides a total of 33 secret locations.

Short and Sweet

Originally, there was only supposed to be one map in Piggy: "House." However, after the experience proved so popular, more and more maps were added.

♡

The "Trick or Treat" item in Brookhaven's Halloween updates is unique because it is the only item in the game that contains real human sounds.

♡

Pistachio is a rare doll pet in Adopt Me! that is no longer available. It was originally named Pinocchio, but was later renamed Pistachio for unknown reasons.

♡

The first three maps in BedWars were Aztec, Blossom, and Glacier.

♡

The section "Which One" in Tower of Hell is the only section where guessing is part of the game. It is also possible to complete this section without jumping.

Finally, the system is haunted

The Halloween event marks an important milestone for Brookhaven, as it is the very first event to be added to the game since its release. Since Brookhaven was released after Easter, there have been no seasonal or special promotions in the game so far. The Halloween event thus heralds a new era for the game world.

Crucifix without a sermon

The crucifix is an item that players use to protect themselves from most hostile entities. Although the developers emphasize that the experience "DOORS" is not intended to convey a religious message, the crucifix appears to be strongly inspired by religion. The shape of the item is a cross, a symbol associated with Christianity. The symbol that appears on the ground when the crucifix is used is even more complex: the crescent moon in the center represents Islam, and the circle around it represents Judaism through the Star of David. Despite these religious symbols, the existence of the crucifix does not mean that the game takes a religious stance. The developers have merely used these elements as inspiration rather than making the game religious. It should also be noted that, strictly speaking, the item is just a simple cross. To be considered a real crucifix, it would have to bear an image of Christ, but this was probably avoided due to Roblox's terms of use.

Four Scoops of Chaos

In the world of Adopt Me!, ice cream is a popular consumable item that you can purchase. Usually, there is a limit to the number of scoops of ice cream you can add. If you try to add a fourth scoop to your ice cream sundae, a warning appears on the screen indicating that "too many scoops" could cause the ice cream to tip over. Interestingly, however, there was one exception to this rule: during the 2023 Summer Festival, and especially when the mini-game "Ice Cream Frenzy" was released, it was briefly possible to create ice cream with four scoops before the usual limit came back into effect.

Creative like a copier?

MeepCity is a Roblox experience created by user "Alexnewtron" that is popular but also quite controversial. Many accuse the game of being a meeting place for online daters – significantly more so than other Roblox games. MeepCity is also said to have cheerfully stolen from Club Penguin and ToonTown: the cute Meeps have almost exactly the same smiley faces as the Puffles from Club Penguin, which a YouTuber has even proven. The background music? Allegedly taken directly from ToonTown – without any credits, although Alexnewtron claimed it was his. Some of the buildings in the game look suspiciously familiar, and when the mini-game MeepCity Racing was released in 2017, many immediately thought of a cheap Mario Kart copy – with similar sounds and driving feel.

Short and Sweet

In the experience "Piggy", there is a special feature regarding the traps: Only the teleporter trap has an effect that directly affects the Piggy instead of affecting the players as usual. The Insolence trap behaves differently: This is the only trap that can affect both the Piggy and the players.

♡

The bed in BedWards is designed to withstand explosions. It cannot be destroyed by TNT, fireballs, or other explosive devices.

♡

The "New Year Event" in Brookhaven is not only the first event of each year, but also the only event that does not start on a Friday.

♡

You cannot dress up, name, or level up the practice dog.

From seed to record holder

Grow a Garden was developed primarily by the development studio Splitting Point Studios, with support from the development studio Do Big Studios. The experience puts you in the role of a gardener who is given a small piece of land. Your task is to plant seeds and care for them carefully until they grow into beautiful flowers, fruits, or vegetables. After harvesting, the produce can be sold to earn "Sheckles," the game's currency. These Sheckles can be used to purchase new seeds, equipment, eggs, and various decorative items to beautify and expand your garden. The experience has proven to be a remarkable success and currently holds several records within the Roblox universe. These include, for example:

- Highest number of visitors in one day: 482,254,488 visits and in one week: 2,052,822,520 visits.
- Highest number of active players in one game: 21,461,453 simultaneously active players.
- Highest number of visitors in one hour: 40,861,829 visits.
- First game to reach 5,000,000, 10,000,000, 15,000,000, and 20,000,000 simultaneous players.
- First standalone game in gaming history to reach 20,000,000 simultaneous players.
- Surpasses Brookhaven in daily number of simultaneous players.
- Has overtaken Fortnite in terms of active players.
- Considered one of the fastest growing games of all time.
- Fastest game to reach 1,000,000,000 visits.

In addition, the success of "Grow a Garden" contributed significantly to Roblox recording the highest number of concurrent players of any video game in a single day.

When hackers get bored...

Some bake cakes, others hack Roblox games: A particularly "creative" hacker named "IHATE23122," better known as Xeno, disrupted several popular games such as Sprunki RP and Classic Parkour between 2024 and 2025 with targeted hacks (so-called exploits). He exploited vulnerabilities in the game code to manipulate functions or crash servers, for example – true to the motto: chaos is also a game mechanic.

Of course, this did not go unnoticed: videos and reports about his actions soon circulated on YouTube, even attracting international attention to the scene. The consequences? Ruined matches, unfair gaming advantages, community disputes, and so-called "rankle" effects – i.e., arguments and stress that continued to simmer in fan forums long after the exploit.

The brain behind the merch

As a fan of the Roblox game Murder Mystery 2, you can now enjoy your own merchandise collection. This includes T-shirts and hoodies, among other items. An exciting detail that many people don't know is that the Roblox character featured on the clothing belongs to none other than "Nikilis", the developer and creative mind behind the popular game. Nikilis is originally from Toronto and, according to an archived profile, has Polish roots.

Roblox rocks the stage

Just as large trade fairs and conferences in the real world share knowledge and showcase innovations, Roblox regularly hosts groundbreaking events that celebrate the immense creativity of its community and provide developers with valuable insights into the future direction of the platform. One annual highlight was the glamorous Bloxy Awards ceremony, which also served as an impressive fundraising event. The virtual mega-event in 2020 captivated 600,000 viewers. Since 2022, the Bloxy Awards have been renamed the Roblox Innovation Awards to continue to recognize outstanding achievements on the platform. For its elite content creators, Roblox Corporation also hosts the exclusive Roblox Developers Conference each year. This three-day event in San Francisco is invitation-only and offers top developers a unique opportunity to learn firsthand about the groundbreaking innovations and developments they can expect on the platform. Similar conferences have already been successfully held in other global cities, such as London.

Short and Sweet

During the 2019 Halloween event, Meeps had vampire teeth, making them rare special versions.

♡

Previously, you could transform into a doctor or patient in the waiting room in MeepCity and into a nurse in the examination room, but this feature has been removed.

♡

The Tix logo was updated in 2017 for unknown reasons, although Tix was already phased out a year earlier in 2016.

♡

In a small detail, the hostile entity "Dupe" from DOORS was teased on the official Twitter profile of "LSPLASH." Fans can discover this revelation by opening the developer's profile picture as a separate file. There, in one of the corners, hides the creature known in the game as a treacherous threat.

Pixel Patents Unlocked

Roblox, led by its current CEO David Baszucki, seems to be not only building a virtual world, but also busy lining up at the patent office. They have secured a total of 15 patents – it's like a secret recipe folder for their technical masterpieces. A patent is basically a "hands off!" sign that prevents others from simply copying or selling their inventions. You can get one for anything clever: from new products to sophisticated processes that make digital life easier. You could almost think they want to secure the recipe for the perfect pixel too.

One-Punch-Man-Action in Roblox

In the Roblox experience "The Strongest Battlegrounds," developed by the studio Yielding Arts, players compete against each other. The game is inspired by the popular anime series One-Punch Man. Players can draw on skills and characters from the original series. The game has undergone several name changes in the past, likely for copyright reasons. Until April 10, 2023, the game was known under names such as Saitama Game, Saitama Battleground, and finally Saitama Battlegrounds.

Short and Sweet

When a friend invites you to a round of DOORS, you will receive a special notification. Instead of a regular game invitation, the invitation will be announced in the message as "Get ready to slurrrr!"

♡

Although most players call it a "cloud rattle," the correct name for this toy is "rainbow rattle."

♡

A Nessie can be seen outside the map in Adopt Me! in the beach party area.

♡

The design of the "Divinia Parks" area in Royale High was mainly carried out by developer "Beeism" and took a total of 35 days to complete.

Maximum health and no mercy

The maximum possible health in Blox Fruits for a player is 15,012. To reach this value, you need 2,650 defense points and at least the Draco V3 ability. In addition, the accessory Leviathan Shield is required. Without any accessories or enhancements, the maximum health is 13,345. An impressive increase is possible: with the Leviathan Shield and the Shark V4's (upgraded) Leviathan Armor, health can even rise to 19,983. If you only use the Leviathan Shield accessory without any further adjustments, the maximum value is 14,345 health points.

When free becomes a cash cow

You might think that free online games hardly generate any profit, right? But Roblox proves the opposite: although it is completely free to play and offers a huge selection of different game modes and experiences, it has already generated over $2 billion in revenue through in-game purchases and its own currency, "Robux." This remarkable success is mainly thanks to players who purchase Robux to customize their avatars, unlock special abilities, or simply support their favorite developers. This has created a system that benefits both players and the company.

Only for sharp eyes

The windows in the secret "Nice View" section of the Tower of Hell game have a hidden feature that is only visible under certain graphics settings. At graphics settings of level 3 or higher, these windows display a gray filter that makes the view outside appear cloudy. Players who leave their graphics settings at level 1 or 2 will not be able to see this special visual feature. Try it out next time you play Tower of Hell ;)

Awakening with a price tag

In real life, developing a groundbreaking product can often involve enormous costs and unforeseen challenges. Roblox experienced something similar when it created a new special ability for one of its characters. Each standard character has a special ability called "Awakening." When activated, the character gains a completely new, significantly more powerful set of moves. However, creating the Awakening for the The Strongest Battlegrounds character "Tech Prodigy" was a real odyssey and significantly delayed an update. The development proved extremely difficult and costly, with expenses exceeding $10,000. The complexity of the animation was so high that many animators rejected it as too time-consuming, forcing the developers to rely on a single artist to complete the entire sequence.

Breaking through walls for advanced learners

With the special attack "Earth-Splitting Strike" of the character "Martial Artist," it is possible to catapult opponents through walls in The Strongest Battlegrounds. This glitch occurs when the opponent is thrown through the air after being hit and "teleports" just before hitting the ground. If players execute this attack near a wall, the opponent flies through the wall after being hit, falls into nothingness, and dies instantly.

Where inspiration meets nightmares

Behind the scenes of the popular horror experience DOORS lies a story marked by creative collaboration and inspiration. In August 2022, the development team "LSPLASH," consisting of "Lightning_Splash" and "RediblesQW" and other supporters 'Ghostly_Wowzers' and "jasper_creations," released a first-person horror game that borrows from other successful horror games. On the one hand, the experience "Rooms" by 'nicorocks5555' served as inspiration, in which players must pass through endless doors and flee from threatening entities in closets. On the other hand, DOORS also bears a remarkable resemblance to the indie horror game "Spooky's Jump Scare Mansion."

A collector's item in a class of its own

Have you ever wondered which virtual collectible is the most coveted and, at the same time, the hardest to get? In the dazzling world of digital creations, there is a helmet that has a very special story behind it. The Kleos Aphthiton was introduced on the Roblox Marketplace on August 27, 2007. Its extreme rarity stems from the fact that it was awarded exclusively to the four best participants in the Grand Melee tournament. As the second edition of the coveted Kleos series, this unique helmet, whose number was limited to eleven copies on February 19, 2017, is now one of the rarest items in existence.

Roblox is redefining gaming

When you think of giants in the gaming world, titles such as "Fortnite", "Minecraft", and "Grand Theft Auto V" often come to mind, each of which inspires millions of players and continually redefines the limits of what is possible in virtual worlds. But while these games boast impressive numbers in terms of player base and revenue, there is one platform that is in a league of its own when it comes to user-generated content: Roblox. With an incredible 71.5 million daily active users and an even more impressive library of 4.4 million active user-created games, referred to by Roblox itself as "experiences," Roblox set an undisputed record as the largest user-generated gaming platform at the end of 2023.

From drops to top yields

There is a proven method for using a master sprinkler in Grow a Garden, known as the sprinkler method. The principle behind it is simple: use any type of sprinkler to accelerate plant growth, maximize their size, and increase the likelihood of mutations. To make this method even more effective, you can combine it with other special sprinklers. The Berry Blush Sprinkler is a good example of this. Certain companions with special abilities, such as Moon Cats, can also further increase the efficiency of this strategy.

Rules of the game? I don't know any, I'm the admin!

In Roblox's "Murder Mystery 2," it is extremely unlikely to be assigned the role of murderer multiple times in a row. The game mechanics are designed so that the probability of becoming the murderer again decreases significantly after each round in which you have held this role. While rare, it is possible to be randomly selected as the murderer twice in a row. However, there is one exception: if you have been granted administrator privileges by "Nikilis", the game's creator, you can bypass this restriction. By using the admin command "/murderer" in the chat, you can repeatedly appoint yourself as the murderer, regardless of the normal game rules.

Short and Sweet

In BedWars, if another player's brewing cauldron is destroyed, the ingredients it contains do not fall to the ground but are placed directly in the inventory of the player who broke the cauldron.

♡

Brookhaven RP won two awards at the 2024 Roblox Innovation Awards: "Best Role-Playing Game/Life Simulation" and "Best Social Hangout."

♡

The ice cream shop in Meep City is based on the unreleased "ToonTown 2.0" prototype, which is basically a nostalgic knockoff suspected of plagiarism with no official mention in the code.

♡

Although it has not yet been officially confirmed, it is estimated that the job "delivery driver" at Pizza Planet is the most frequently played job in Welcome to Bloxburg.

Technology plays tricks on us

After Erik Cassel died, some strange things happened on his Roblox account. In May 2014 in particular, many players noticed that his account was suddenly back online. This raised questions and led to many speculations. Some thought that a hacker had taken over the account. Others believed that perhaps his younger brother or his children were using it. Most assumed that it was indeed his children. On October 8, 2023, Erik's account was once again displayed as "online." This time, however, it was just a system error that caused many old accounts to appear active by mistake.

More than just a classroom

Brookhaven School, the high school in Brookhaven, has several interesting and little-known features: One of these features is the school's own skate park. This was originally located under the bridge near the former site of the Burger Barn (now the Entertainment Center), but has since been integrated into the school. Furthermore, the school offers a unique customization option: in each classroom, both the blackboards and the screens can be individually modified. A particularly hidden detail is a secret room behind the auditorium. From there, a ladder leads directly to the skate park.

Four wheels, one legend

In the experience "Welcome to Bloxburg", vehicles are the most important means of transportation. There is a special vehicle that is solely owned by the developer Coeptus and is usually referred to by the gaming community as the "monster truck." This vehicle, which is basically a Roat 500 with significantly oversized wheels, has been described by players who have seen it in action as the fastest in the entire game. However, it is not possible to buy this monster truck or obtain it in any other way.

Brown in the picture, colorful on the shelf

You are standing in the library. The silence is eerie. Your heart is pounding. You have only one chance to escape from this creepy room. You know that the books are the key. You see the symbol depicting the brown books and begin your search. You comb through every shelf, but the brown books seem not to exist. At that moment, you realize that, ironically, the truth comes in a different guise: the brown books shown on the symbol in the Roblox experience "DOORS" do not exist in that color in the game. Nevertheless, the books you find in the library are collectible items that are crucial to solving the puzzle and finding your way to freedom.

Brazilian-style maze fun

The Brazilian Cube, often simply referred to as the BR Cube, is a unique cube decorated with the Brazilian flag on all sides. It is most likely an Easter egg that the developers introduced as a sign of appreciation for the Brazilian Blox Fruits player community.

Currently, the cube serves purely decorative purposes. The Brazil Cube features the words "Que Isso," which can be translated as "What is this?" In the past, administrators could summon the cube.

If a player touched the cube, they were teleported to a maze. Upon successfully completing the maze, they received a free Dark Blade as a reward.

This special ability to obtain a Dark Blade only worked when the cube was spawned by an administrator. This feature is no longer known to all admins, and Rip_indra is currently the only one known to still be able to perform this action.

Short and Sweet

The "Station" map in RIVALS has an interesting history. It was originally designed by developer "GreatGuyBoom" as a lobby for a battle royale game. In early 2024, the map was extensively reworked and integrated into RIVALS as a standalone map.

It takes about 22 seconds to harvest a blueberry in Grow a Garden. A full harvest, i.e., a complete harvest area, is only ready for harvesting after 105 seconds.

In the Xbox version and on Android smartphones, it is not possible to purchase and use radios in Murder Mystery 2. This feature is only available on PCs and Android and iPad tablets.

The "Castle" and "Castle Grounds" maps in BedWars are identical.

Nature Meditation 2.0

Some people find deep relaxation in observing nature—be it a fish in an aquarium or a bird in a cage. But imagine if there was a place where the pure joy of synchronized dancing took center stage: In the diverse world of Roblox, there is an experience called "Dancing Parrots" where players can exclusively watch parrots dancing in sync.

A real brain rot

Can a game test you so much that you feel like bursting into tears? That's exactly what happens in "Steal a Brainrot." This online game is about stealing other players' Brainrots—strange creatures generated by AI, some of which look like sharks wearing Nike shoes. Although stealing is the core of the game, many young players are overwhelmed by the consequences.

In 2025, videos went viral on TikTok showing children breaking down in tears when their beloved Brainrot was stolen. One of the most famous clips shows a crying boy whose sister then swears revenge and has been viewed over 36 million times. The game itself is merciless: the environment is spartan, with only cages, assembly lines for new Brainrots, and short shields. To get the best items, you have to spend real money, which can mean up to $50 for admin rights.

Short and Sweet

Diamond Beach in Royale High owes its name to the often astonishing number of diamonds that can be collected on the beach.

♡

Chapter 3 in Piggy was created before Chapter 2.

♡

Pets can be fed with an empty green tea cup in Adopt Me! to complete their "Thirsty" task.

♡

When looking at BedWard's character "Zeno," it is noticeable that he wears a chain with a key attached to it. This key bears a striking resemblance to that of the Spirit Catcher. The only visual difference between the two keys is the way they glow.

Explosive fun with Death Adder style

Death Adder is a kit in BedWars with the special ability to collect alchemy shards and fire them as projectiles. These projectiles are capable of destroying blocks and launching enemies into the air. The name and design of Death Adder are inspired by the venomous snake of the same name, which is one of the most poisonous land animals in Australia. A notable detail of the Comet ability is that it actually deals double damage, which often goes unnoticed. When it hits directly, the comet itself causes ranged damage. The subsequent explosion then deals additional explosion damage. This double damage effect can be seen in the kill feed when a player is eliminated by the comet.

How Winx Club enchanted Roblox

Who would have thought that a television series would provide the basis for one of the most popular role-playing games on Roblox? Royale High, created by developer "callmehbob" and her team, has its roots in the magical world of Winx Club. As a big fan, she wanted to develop a game that would allow players to experience a magical school life as a fairy, mermaid, or other mythical creature.

Cold shock of prices

The "Dominus Frigidus" is an exceptionally rare and unique hat. It consists of a light blue hood with a black interior that completely conceals the wearer's face. The shoulder rings are also light blue with gray exteriors to match. A striking detail are the feathers, which are shaped like icicles and give the hat a frosty appearance. As of October 31, 2023, Dominus Frigidus ranked first among all items on the platform in terms of its recent average price. This high average price is largely due to a historic sale: in December 2022, mr_beanGuy, the creator of the Ragdoll engine, purchased a copy from Bourgist, another developer, for an incredible 200 million Robux. To date, this trade marks the largest sale of a limited-edition item in the history of Roblox.

Change quickly, live long

If you change your race during combat in Blox Fruits, this does not count as death. Even if your opponent had met the necessary requirements to receive a bounty or honor, the game will simply end the battle and ignore the process. This means that the bounty counter will not change. This is because changing races causes the player to reappear immediately, rather than killing them first and then reviving them.

Short and Sweet

Mr. P's last name is "Poppyseed," as evidenced by the official Mr. P plush toy.

♡

The "Glass Cannon" in RIVALS has a special feature. It differs from all other weapons in that it can only fire a single bullet. Another special feature is that it can never achieve headshots, regardless of how accurately you aim.

♡

Unlike marines, pirates in Blox Fruits cannot start a quest to defeat the player with a bounty by clicking on their wanted poster.

♡

Mature pepper plants in Grow a Garden can bear up to six fruits at a time, with three fruits developing on each of the two shoots. This characteristic also applies to the dragon pepper variety.

Money doesn't grow on trees - or does it?

You know the money tree as a popular decorative item in the game Adopt Me!, which can be purchased in the furniture catalog under the "Rare" section for 1,450 bucks.

Originally, the money tree dispensed 5 bucks every thirty minutes. However, this feature was improved in an update, so that players now receive 8 bucks for the same period of time.

However, the ability to generate unlimited money by owning multiple money trees was removed from Adopt Me! through a bug fix update. The developers justified this move by saying that it would have been too easy for players to collect unlimited amounts of in-game currency. Even if players own multiple money trees today, they cannot collect more than the specified maximum amount of money per day.

A world map full of gaps

The digital world is limitless – or is it? Although we often assume that online experiences are globally accessible, there are exceptions. Roblox is blocked or banned in several countries. This currently affects China, Jordan, North Korea, Oman, and Turkey. In Turkey, the ban was imposed due to content that could promote gambling or child sexual abuse. Furthermore, the platform was inaccessible in the United Arab Emirates from 2018 to 2021, and Guatemala issued a parental warning in 2021. There are also specific restrictions in Belgium and the Netherlands: certain games on this platform have been restricted due to regulations on so-called "loot boxes" in order to protect children from gambling risks (as of July 2025).

The hunt for 1,375,000 XP

Battle Passes were introduced to BedWars on August 27, 2021, and have been the primary method of earning rewards in the game ever since. Each season typically lasts 16 weeks, but at least 8 weeks. Players can unlock a variety of rewards by reaching different levels in the Battle Pass. These include titles, emotes, dance emotes, kill effects, lobby gadgets, kit skins, Golden Lucky Chests, and Diamond Lucky Chests. Kits were also available as rewards in the past.
To complete the entire Battle Pass, players must collect a total of 1,375,000 XP. It's interesting to note that by level 37 or 38, you've already collected about half of the experience points required.

Explosive ascent to the viewpoint

You can climb the crane on the "Construction" map in RIVALS to gain a strategic advantage. You can do this by using an RPG or a grenade. The explosion will propel you towards the crane. Once you're close enough, activate your character's "Scythe" ability to dash the rest of the way. Even if you're not at the top yet, you'll land on the crane's boom. Climb up from there and use Scythe again to reach the top.

Although the map has a lot of strategic potential, it is unpopular with many players. The main reason for this is that opponents with activated aim assist and auto-shoot functions, which are common on consoles and mobile devices, camp on the crane with a sniper rifle.

Some players also use a riot shield to protect themselves from damage from the front or rear.

Winter without end

Many players are familiar with the typical pattern: November brings snow, March takes it away. But that has changed. For a long time, Brookhaven RP followed a familiar rhythm: the first snow usually came in November, but disappeared right on time at the beginning of spring at the end of March. This seasonal consistency was almost part of the game's identity. But 2025 surprised everyone with a significant deviation. The snow remained until the end of April – much longer than usual. This caused astonishment and speculation in the community: Was it intentional or a mistake? One possible reason for the extended snow season is the takeover of the game by Canadian development studio Voldex. Since then, the game calendar seems to have shifted slightly – perhaps inspired by the real, long winters of Canada. In any case, there has never been snow in Brookhaven as long as in 2025.

Mikedop sends greetings from Bloxburg

In Welcome to Bloxburg, there are a variety of headlines on the news channel that can appear as breaking news. One of these reports is quite special, as it reads: "Mikedop was here." This is a reference to Mikedop, a good friend of Bloxburg developer Coeptus and one of the contributors to the game.

New bed, same battle

Can a game concept inspire an entire community twice? BedWars is living proof that it can. This popular Roblox experience, developed by the game developer group "Easy.gg," was released in beta in May 2021. The strategic challenge of defending your own bed and destroying those of the opposing teams has proven to be an absolute hit and has built up a huge fan base. It's an impressive remake of the original BedWars, which was already a legend on Hypixel's Minecraft platform.

The Communication World of Roblox

In real life, there are rules that ensure we can interact in a safe environment. Roblox handles this in a similar way, offering you a variety of ways to communicate with other players, whether through in-game chat or private messages. However, not all features are immediately available to everyone. For example, voice chat is only accessible to players over the age of 13 who have verified their age. You can also only use direct messages without restrictions if you are 13 years of age or older. Younger players can only use this feature if they have received explicit permission from their parents.

All checks given to you as a player in Welcome to Bloxburg bear the signature of "Mr. Blox." However, the identity of this person is unknown.

Short and Sweet

The "Blobsaw" skin for the chainsaw in RIVALS is a reference to the character Pochita from the manga and anime series Chainsaw Man.

Guns cannot harm rubber users in any way, even with Aura.

In the world of Bloxburg, time always starts on a new server or in a newly created neighborhood on Monday morning at 8:00 a.m.

By killing all bosses with the quest in Blox Fruits, you will earn approximately $ 165,000 in the first sea, $ 170,001 in the second sea, and $ 247,500 in the third sea (without 2x money).

Roblox conquers the US

Just as playing outdoors or meeting at the youth center used to be part of everyday life, today there is a digital meeting place that is invaluable to young people in the US: according to the company, more than half of all Americans under the age of 16 spend their time on Roblox. Among children aged 9 to 12, three out of four actively use this popular platform.

Diary Detective

In Piggy, the Player's Journal serves as a mechanism that tells the story from the perspective of the player character. It provides insight into the character's thoughts and feelings during cutscenes and describes how they perceive the events. To unlock the individual entries in this diary, players must find all the pages hidden in the chapters of Piggy: Book 1 and Piggy: Book 2. An interesting detail is that the names of chapters 10 to 12 of Book 2 are displayed as "???" if the corresponding diary entries have not yet been unlocked. A plausible explanation for this is that this mechanic was introduced when the game was only released up to Chapter 9 of Book 2. In order not to spoil future content for players, the names of the following chapters were deliberately hidden. It is suspected that "MiniToon," the game's developer, either forgot to add the names after the release of the last chapters or did not have time to do so.

The twin berries from Grow Garden

The celestiberry and the raspberry in Grow a Garden look very similar because both fruits use the same 3D model. The plant on which the celestiberry grows also has an interesting history: it shares its model with the scrapped crimson vine, a plant that was originally planned for the Blood Moon event. The only difference between the two models is the color scheme: while the crimson vine was red, the celestiberry is exclusively shades of blue.

From wise to spicy

A cosmetic item called "Grilled Moon Owl" was distributed to all Grow a Garden players shortly before the "Bizzier Bees" update was released. This happened because the developer "Jandel" jokingly announced in the hours before the Bizzier Bees event update that the Wise Owl would reappear later, grilled on a barbecue. Jandel activated two nights in a row at that time. Since the inventory in both "Twilight Shops" was poor, he decided to give players the grilled moon owl as a cosmetic item. It was originally planned to make this owl available as a pet for all players.

Short and Sweet

You know the "L'Église de Prophétie" (English: The Church of Prophecy) in Blox Fruits as the place where you can awaken your Blox Fruit after a raid. There is a little secret there: The words "Life form" on the left side are a so-called Easter egg and a direct reference to the Dark Blade's Slayer Skin.

♡

When a hero shoots an innocent person, both die.

♡

Hunger is the mood in Welcome to Bloxburg that deteriorates the fastest. In contrast, hygiene declines the slowest.

♡

Figure, one of the most important enemy entities in DOORS, has been modeled after the sandworm from the movie "Dune", particularly in terms of its appearance, head, and facial features.

Short and Sweet

If you see a blocked account or have problems with the Roblox website, the Robux icon will appear with a question mark.

Sparky is the fastest NPC in Piggy.

Royale High was originally called "Fairies and Mermaids Winx High School."

The Red Cardinal has similar animations to the Bird of Paradise.

The tsuba, or guard of the blade, of Blade Master in The Strongest Battlegrounds is designed to resemble an atom.

There is a button hidden in the coffin in Brookhaven Church that will teleport you. You will also see a picture of Mr. Brookhaven in the coffin.

A Kamui trick that caught the eye

In Blox Fruits, certain abilities, known as "admin abilities," are exclusively available to developers and administrators. These special functions often manifest themselves in the form of items in the hotbar, specific commands, or unique locations in the game. A well-known YouTuber named "SilentAsura" once obtained the "Rip Kamui" ability as a prize for winning an event hosted by an administrator. However, he exploited this ability in an unauthorized manner. The "Rip Kamui" allowed him to teleport other players directly from a safe zone to the "Rip Family Hideout." Asura abused this feature to hunt players for bounties there. As a result of this misconduct, his account was suspended and the ability was permanently revoked.

Pixels on the Trading Floor

While Wall Street was busy with stocks and bonds, the gaming world had its own fascinating parallel world of trading. From 2008 to 2016, players could trade their internal currencies—Robux and the then-called Tickets—on a special platform called RoblEX, just like on a real stock exchange. This system gave users the opportunity to speculate cleverly and increase their wealth by trading these two currencies. With the abolition of tickets, this spectacle finally came to an end in April 2016.

Aging is not for beginners

In real life, we grow not only in years but also in experience. We learn every new hobby and skill quickly at first, but over time it becomes more difficult to reach new heights. It's very similar in the "Welcome to Bloxburg" experience. Here, too, the time required to gain a new skill point depends on the rank already achieved in the respective skill. The higher you climb in rank, the more time is needed to reach the next level. For example, at level 7, it takes 50 seconds to gain a skill point if you have activated a +++ effect.

LEVEL UP!

Growth that knows no bounds?

The Eldertree is a unique kit in BedWards with a special ability: it can absorb tree orbs. Instead of increasing defense, this increases its size and maximum health. Although there is a theoretical upper limit for health points, it is difficult to determine. It depends on how many players are affected by the kit's "Forest" ability. Ultimately, the limit depends on when a server is forced to restart, assuming perfect internet connections and gaming devices. However, assuming that Roblox servers automatically shut down after two days, it would theoretically be possible to reach over a million health points. For comparison, the current record is significantly lower, at around 3,000 health points.

Short and Sweet

Lake Madison is the only place in Brookhaven with working water.

♡

The research facility has the most interactive features of all the maps in Murder Mystery 2.

♡

On Twitch, Royale High developer “Callmehbob” streamed the entire development of the “Beach House” area so that people could see the work in progress.

♡

The Oaks community is the only community in Brookhaven without a subway station.

♡

Before Roblox existed, David Baszucki, aka “builderman,” was active on the radio from an early age. He had his own talk show while he was still in school.

Short and Sweet

When feeding pets in the experience "Grow a Garden", sometimes a long combination of numbers and letters (called a UUID, which appears in curly brackets) appears in the interaction prompt instead of their actual names.

Crafting is one of the basic features in Murder Mystery 2. The weapons displayed in the crafting icon are Seer, Hallow's Edge, Fang, and Tides.

Modern Mansion is one of the largest mansions in Brookhaven.

Deep in the ventilation shafts of the police station, you will find a secret room with a key card hidden behind a cabinet. This key card opens the Brookhaven Electric building.

Short and Sweet

Initially, when players approached the character "Piggy", a familiar piece of music would play: the theme song from Peppa Pig. However, to create a threatening atmosphere, it was slowed down and distorted. Due to copyright concerns, the melody was later removed from the game and replaced with another.

♡

At the 2024 Roblox Innovation Awards, Blox Fruits was awarded the prize in the "Best Action/RPG" category.

♡

The name "Draco" for the species in Blox Fruits comes from the Latin word for dragon.

Curved, popular, but not stronger

Have you ever wondered if the Karambit skin in RIVALS is really better? Its distinctive curved design, based on the traditional Indonesian karambit, has made it a favorite among many players. Despite its cool appearance and rumors of a larger hitbox, its hit area is identical to that of all other knife skins. The supposedly greater range that you sometimes feel is actually mostly due to a poor internet connection.

Lua, Click & Boom

Roblox uses a programming language called Lua, which is designed to be simple and easy to understand. Many children and teenagers take their first steps in programming with it, without any prior knowledge. With Lua, you can determine what happens when you click a button, open a box, or use a secret teleporter, for example. But don't worry: you don't have to be a math genius to do this. Many developers have taught themselves everything they know using YouTube videos, Roblox Studio, and a little patience.

The best part? Many famous Roblox games were made by young people – some even earn real money from them. If you work hard at programming, you can become a game designer on Roblox. Maybe there's a little developer or future developer in you too.

Short and Sweet

Initially, Piggy lacked the ability to highlight interactive objects with tooltips. However, this was changed later on, as many players had difficulty understanding what actions were possible and often felt disoriented.

As a player, you can only join the same custom Bedwars game up to three times per account.

The space for pets in the inventory in Grow a Garden is limited to 60. Players who want to keep more pets can expand this capacity by trading in aged pets.

On April 1, 2020, in keeping with April Fools' Day, the title of the experience "Welcome to Bloxburg" was renamed "House Building Simulator". As part of this change, the preview image of the game was also replaced.

The Robux Standard

Similar to the early days of money, when barter currencies such as cowrie shells or precious metals existed alongside coins that were introduced later, there was also a dual system in the world of Roblox. In addition to the paid Robux, players used the free Tix (tickets) to shop on the marketplace. On April 14, 2016, this coexistence came to an abrupt end. Tix were abolished by Roblox and all remaining player credits expired – a historic currency reform in the virtual world. Since then, the main currency Robux has been the only way to pay in the game.

Make way for the coolest ice cream truck

It sounds contradictory, but sometimes a rail vehicle has to come into play to transform a road vehicle. In March 2020, an originally spartan ice cream truck, which initially only had room for its driver, received a surprising upgrade: with the introduction of the Choo Choo Train in Adopt Me!, an additional seat was added. This unexpected connection made the vehicle an absolute exception, as it is the only game that can offer players all kinds of food.

Whoever tames the dragon rules the game

Only a few players will ever be lucky enough to find the legendary dragon fruit. In Blox Fruits, it is considered the most expensive and hardest to obtain fruit in the entire game. Those who possess it can transform themselves into a powerful dragon – with the largest player model in the game. The design of the dragon forms is particularly fascinating, as it borrows heavily from mythology: the Eastern variant is strongly reminiscent of a long, a traditional Chinese mythical creature, while the Western form is modeled after a wyvern, a winged dragon from European mythology. An interesting contrast to tradition can be seen in their abilities: in Chinese myths, dragons are considered rulers of water, wind, and thunder – powerful beings that control the weather and the seas. In the game, however, the Eastern dragon relies primarily on fiery attacks – an ironic reversal of traditional elements.

Short and Sweet

Among all the light sources in the game DOORS, the candle has a special feature: it is the only one that displays a message to the player when its fuel is exhausted. Neither the lighter nor the flashlight provide such feedback. When the candle goes out, the message “Your Candle ran out” appears.

♡

In Grow a Garden, certain plants may receive a very high price of 1 trillion due to an unusually high number of mutations. This phenomenon is considered a bug. Examples of plants that may be affected include the Spiked Mango and the Bone Blossom.

♡

In February 2025, a Roblox programming camp for children aged 10 to 13 took place in Berlin, Germany.

A classic reissue

The Tower of Hell, often abbreviated as "TToH," is the second release from the development studio "YXCeptional Studios." While similar to the original "Tower of Hell," it differs in that it features a fixed sequence of 17 'vanilla' sections created by developer "ObrenTune," which are considered the original levels of the game. Unlike the original, which offers 6 to 12 randomly arranged sections, TToH focuses on a predefined gaming experience. This version of the game deliberately omits elements such as mutators, gears, or a timer. The developers wanted to create a simplified, classic version of Tower of Hell that is more accessible to players and perceived as much easier than the main game. It thus offers a return to the roots of the game's concept.

League of BedWars

It seems as though the developers of BedWars have borrowed some of their mechanics from the well-known game "League of Legends." Particularly striking is the similarity between the character 'Kaida' and the champion "Illaoi" from League of Legends. Their abilities are suspiciously similar. Another parallel can be found in Nazar, whose abilities bear a strong resemblance to Lee Sin, another champion from League of Legends. It seems reasonable to assume that the developers were deliberately inspired by these champions.

Roblox's user base is made up of 44% female users and 56% male users, which represents a nearly even split.

Playfully rich

In the dynamic world of Roblox, some game developers have built up considerable fortunes through their creativity and dedication. By monetizing their games with the virtual currency Robux, which can be exchanged for real money, many developers have managed to turn their passion into a lucrative profession. The numbers speak for themselves: in 2022 alone, Roblox paid out over $500 million to its developers. This impressive sum highlights the immense potential of Roblox game development and the success of many developers who have been able to realize their dreams.

From beta to legend

Originally known as "Classic: Rocket Arena," this experience holds a special place in Roblox history as the oldest experience ever released on the platform. Its origins date back to January 2006, a time when Roblox was still in beta. Rocket Arena was a free battle arena where players competed against each other. This concept served as inspiration for numerous later popular Roblox titles. Despite its historical significance, Rocket Arena, along with many other early official Roblox games,was discontinued in 2017. The exact reasons for the shutdown remain unknown to this day.

No Dictionary Required

Imagine making a new friend on Roblox, chatting and joking around in an exciting experience, only to realize that your friend has been writing in Korean the whole time and you've been writing in German, and neither of you noticed! This is possible because Roblox uses special AI that instantly translates messages in chat. This technology works between 16 languages, including English, Spanish, French, Korean, German, and many more. This allows children and adults from all over the world to understand each other without a dictionary or translation app. It makes it easy to make new friends and go on adventures together, no matter where you come from or what language you speak.

Trash + raccoon = rash

We all know those clever little raccoons that rummage through trash cans at night. This typical trait gave the developer of the Roblox experience Piggy a special idea. He was looking for a name for his raccoon character that would suit the animal. The name Rash is the result of some creative thinking: it starts with an "R" like in "raccoon," but also refers to the word "trash," which is a funny reference to the animal's lifestyle.

On March 11, 2011, the limited edition "Purple Indy" hat disappeared from the Roblox Marketplace in record time. It sold out in just 5 seconds, making it the fastest-selling limited edition hat in Roblox history.

Short and Sweet

The accessory "Whimsy Witch Hexed Bodice" stands out because it is the only item in a set that offers more variations for male characters than for female characters.

The section "Spiky Cylinder" was formerly called "Pink Cylinder," but its name was changed because the section was recolored and is no longer pink.

The Sorcerer is the character with the shortest cooldowns in The Strongest Battlegrounds, ranging from 2 to 10 seconds.

Orion Offensive was a popular Roblox clan founded in July 2015. Within a few months, it grew to over 40,000 members – then it was unexpectedly closed in September 2017 because the founders left Roblox.

Pixel nostalgia

Tetris, the legendary puzzle game from 1984, has been keeping players busy for decades, rotating and stacking falling blocks to form perfect rows. This iconic game concept is reflected, at least in name, in "Tetris Game Night," a secret section of "ObrenTune" in Tower of Hell, which also pays homage to another classic game with a giant Pong screen. This special section brings together two icons of video game history: Pong from 1972, considered one of the first commercially successful video games, and Tetris, the puzzle phenomenon of the 1980s. In addition to this double retro reference, Tetris Game Night also stands out visually, as it is one of the few colored sections in the entire game, a rare and eye-catching highlight in the otherwise monochrome tower.

The dough that lives with you

The pizza dough is an interactable furniture item in Adopt Me! that provides you with an unlimited supply of homemade pizza. This food item replenishes your "hunger" status. One advantage of the pizza dough is that the pizza made with it remains in your inventory even if you leave the game and start again later. Beyond simply providing pizza, pizza dough allows you to further personalize the homemade pizza you have collected. You can add various toppings to these pizzas and then prepare them to suit your taste.

Short and Sweet

In the "RIVALS" experience, there is a map called "Bridge," which is located in the South Korean capital of Seoul. It is believed that the setting is specifically modeled after the Hangang Bridge.

♡

One way to team up with a pirate as a marine in Blox Fruits is to join one of their raids. This alliance cannot be broken while the raid is ongoing. The alliance with one or more pirates is automatically terminated as soon as the player dies or resets their character.

♡

The "Safari Egg" in Adopt Me! was the shortest-lived of all the eggs from the "Gumball Machine," available for only 57 days.

♡

Murder Mystery 2 is not only the title of the popular Roblox experience, but also the name of a crime comedy of the same name that was released in 2023.

When cogs become meeps

Some things in life are so good that they inspire us to create something similar, perhaps even something that takes the original idea further. That could well be the case with MeepCity. The developer "alexnewtron," who created the experience on Roblox, was previously a fairly active member of the Toontown Rewritten community. Toontown Rewritten is a free, fan-made remake of the discontinued MMORPG Disney's Toontown Online, in which you create a Toon (a cartoon character) to save a crazy world from robot-like villains called "Cogs." The similarities are striking: many of the features in MeepCity, such as fishing, gardening, and the party system, are very reminiscent of Toontown's gameplay. Some fans even think it's been copied almost shamelessly.

From Oofish to baby talk

The "Welcome to Bloxburg" experience offers an unusual feature that allows you to customize the display of the game text. In the settings menu, under the language selection, you will find a list that includes four special options in addition to the usual languages. These alternative settings change the entire text display in the game in creative ways. Robonesisch replaces all letters and words with random numbers. Oofisch replaces the entire text with different spellings of the word "Oof." If you select Aliensch, all letters are accented, making them look unusual. The Babysprache option ensures that all text is displayed in the style of toddler language.

Short and Sweet

When a "standard gorilla box" is opened, there is a party balloon animation in which several colorful party balloons pop out.

♡

Every month, 64 million people gather in the colorful world of Roblox, across all devices.

♡

The camper van was the first vehicle in Brookhaven that you could stand up in.

♡

The effect that occurs when breaking a lucky block can determine the rarity of the drop.

♡

If you find yourself on the cursed ship at night in Blox Fruits, transforming into the unawakened Buddha will help you see a little better in the darkness.

The in-game name of Erik Cassel, co-founder of Roblox, is "erik.cassel." His children's Roblox usernames are "stunshocker" and "redustion."

Luxury comes at a price

The "VIP Package" is one of a total of 15 game passes in Brookhaven and offers you a range of exclusive benefits that will significantly enhance your gaming experience. With this package, you benefit from immediate access to houses without having to wait. Vehicle spawning is also accelerated, which means you have shorter waiting times. On public servers, the VIP package allows you to spawn two cars or two boats at the same time, giving you more flexibility and options. Furthermore, you get access to special VIP props and are highlighted in chat with a specially marked VIP tag. At a price of 999 Robux, it is currently the most expensive Game Pass in the game. The "Vehicle Upgrade Pass," on the other hand, is the cheapest pass at 30 Robux.

No tricks, just luck

The Blox Fruits Dealer Cousin has been replaced by Blox Fruit Gacha, a special shop character in the game. He offers players the opportunity to obtain Blox Fruits. Many players believe that they can improve their chances of obtaining rare or powerful fruits by entering certain "secret commands" in the chat before "rolling," such as "/OPluck." However, it has been found that these commands have no effect on the outcome. The allocation of Blox Fruits is entirely random, based purely on luck.

Short and Sweet

The elephant ears from Grow a Garden are based on the mature leaves of the Pink China variety of the plant "Colocasia esculenta".

♡

On the new campus at Royale High, you can find diamonds outside the windows of the art studio.

♡

The Wizard Tower has a total of 12 spots where you can plant flowers. These spots offer enough space to design your own little garden.

♡

"Corrupt" is the only unique weapon that can be traded in Murder Mystery 2.

♡

Yeti is the first and currently only fruit in Blox Fruits that begins with the letter "Y."

As rare as winning the lottery

The Black Iron Crown of Pwnage is an extremely rare and historic accessory in Roblox, introduced in 2007 as the first item in the Black Iron series. It is considered one of the most coveted collectibles, as it was never sold regularly but only awarded to the "godlike deadly warriors," and its rarity was further enhanced by the termination of many original user accounts.

For example, the player "PokerGod" received the accessory for achieving 10,000 knockouts, the player "ColbyValentinoCrown" for reporting security vulnerabilities in Roblox, and the player "AlexVa"lentinoCrown for pointing out numerous bugs and vulnerabilities.

An amusing detail is that the Black Iron Crown used to contain a script called "TelamonTools." This script ensured that "Administrator Phil," another crown owner, was guaranteed to be selected as the murderer for 4,000 seconds every round when he wore it in the experience "Murder Mystery 2".

Out of Air, Out of Time

How long can you hold your breath? In the world of DOORS, the time you can hold your breath determines your fate. Your survival depends on a limited supply of oxygen. If it drops to zero, your adventure is irrevocably over. In the mine air chamber, you only have 52.7 seconds to breathe, while flooding reduces this to just 21.25 seconds. Contact with Seeks Goop at the dam is particularly treacherous: you only have 3.35 seconds left – but you'll usually be fatally wounded before then. Only when hit by Sally do you not have to worry about your life, as oxygen loss is never fatal here. Fortunately, your supply slowly replenishes when you are safe. A completely empty tank is fully replenished after 15.4 seconds.

Form killstreaks like it's nothing

Have you ever wondered how to get killstreaks really fast in The Strongest Battlegrounds without getting slaughtered in hours of combat? In Build Mode, an exclusive feature for private servers+, you have full control over the placement and customization of objects. One of the most useful applications is for quickly farming killstreaks. Simply equip the "Zombie Staff," summon zombies, set the damage to 10x, and defeat them with the "Whirlwind Drop" technique. Each zombie defeated this way counts as one kill, and 10 kills equal a killstreak.

Roblox under criticism

In a world where apps and games are ubiquitous, many parents rely on the protective mechanisms and guidance provided by app and game developers. However, not all parents feel adequately informed. In July 2025, a mother from California sued Roblox because her 12-year-old child was allegedly so addicted to the game that they had to seek psychological help and often had uncontrollable tantrums. She blamed Roblox for the child's poor grades, difficult friendships, and stress at home. She demanded that Roblox should have better informed parents about the possible effects of the game on children's behavior and development.

Full speed ahead with brains

MeepCity Racing is a mini-game in MeepCity that is very reminiscent of Mario Kart. You can drive different karts, all of which accelerate at different speeds. There are three cool tracks: Toybox, Pyramids, and Melody. The Melody track was added during the "Coco" event and is inspired by the Music Park track from Mario Kart 7 and 8. The special thing is that some karts are better than others on certain tracks, so you have to think carefully about which kart to choose! A funny bug even used to allow players to drive through walls on the Toybox track, but that was quickly fixed, of course. This makes racing twice as much fun!

When astronomy meets Roblox horror

What lies behind the glowing lights that guide you through the terrifying halls of DOORS? Much more than just a point of orientation. The mysterious "Three Architects," sometimes referred to as the "Three Lights," are central, enigmatic figures in the Roblox experience "DOORS." These beings—the Guiding Light, the Curious Light, and an unnamed Red Light—appear as glowing entities. Their official name, "Three Architects," comes from a secret message that appears when a crucifix is used against one of them. The crucifix's banishing seal hides an encrypted message in Wingdings font that reads: "One of The Three Architects marked by celestials assists you." This reference to the architects being "marked" by celestial beings suggests that their symbols represent astronomical objects. This fits perfectly with the Guiding Light, whose symbol is reminiscent of the moon, and the Curious Light, which is symbolized by a star. The symbol of the Red Architect is less clear, but could represent a spiral-shaped celestial formation, such as a galaxy, a nebula, or a black hole. A black hole is the most likely interpretation. Many galaxies are spiral-shaped, but not all, which limits the theory. In addition, all known spiral galaxies, including our own Milky Way, have a supermassive black hole at their center, which underscores the connection between these two celestial bodies.

Short and Sweet

Unlike all other characters, the Awakening ability remains permanently active for The Strongest Hero and KJ in The Strongest Battleground once it has been triggered.

♡

There are over 40 million different games (experiences) on the Roblox gaming platform.

♡

Roblox does not have an official Twitch channel, but many creators regularly stream Roblox content for thousands of fans.

♡

In Welcome to Bloxburg, turning off all electrical appliances in your house has no effect on your bills. Instead, the amount of your bills is determined solely by the value of your house and the number of solar panels you have installed.

Hey, hey, hey – who's hatching there

In the world of Adopt Me!, the birth of animals is unique: unlike in reality, where only certain species hatch from eggs, in this game every pet comes from an egg. So if you want to take in a new animal, the first step is always to buy an egg. The type of egg you purchase determines which animal will ultimately hatch from it. There are 5 different classes of animals. These are common, uncommon, rare, ultra rare, and legendary. The more expensive the egg, the rarer the pet.

The secret to big rewards in Piggy

Anyone who completes a level in Piggy on Hard Mode receives 10 additional Piggy Tokens. Without this setting, you would receive 15 tokens, so the reward increases to a total of 25 tokens. This makes Hard Mode a useful way to collect tokens. It becomes particularly rewarding if you have the x2 Piggy Tokens Gamepass and complete a Swarm map on Hard Mode. In this case, you earn 100 tokens. Without the Gamepass, you would receive 55 tokens. The introduction of Hard Mode was hinted at by “MiniToon”, the game's developer, in a tweet before release.

Sonic races to Roblox Olympus

"Sonic Speed Simulator" is a Roblox game based on the iconic blue hedgehog Sonic and has reached a special milestone: with an impressive 933.65 million visits (as of April 25, 2024), it has catapulted itself to the top of the most visited brand-based games on the platform. This extraordinary figure underscores the enduring appeal of Sonic and his fast-paced gameplay within the Roblox community. The popularity of "Sonic Speed Simulator" reflects how well the fast-paced action and familiar universe of the Sega mascot resonate with young players. The game even surpasses other well-known brands. Incidentally, "Miraculous RP: Ladybug & Cat Noir" ranks second among the most visited brand games.

A bumpy road

In Roblox's "Tower of Hell," the path to builder status used to be almost as strictly regulated as a real building permit: first, the submitted sections had to be carefully reviewed and approved by the responsible supervisors before being forwarded to the well-known reviewer "uwuPyxl" in a second round. Only when both instances gave their approval was a player officially allowed to bear the coveted Builder status – a complex procedure that is no longer officially used today.

Short and Sweet

There is no fixed release date for updates to Welcome to Bloxburg. New content and improvements will only be released once they have been fully developed and are ready.

In 2024, Roblox Corporation generated over $3.6 billion in revenue. This is significantly more than in the previous year, when revenue stood at $2.8 billion.

In Welcome to Bloxburg, the status effects stand out from other game features due to a number of linguistic shortcomings. Many of the descriptions contain both grammatical and typographical errors, which sets them apart from the otherwise flawless presentation of the game.

The RIVALS developer's favorite map is "Construction," while the least popular is Onyx.

Short and Sweet

The crocodile was the first reptile pet in Adopt Me!.

♡

Sea beasts in Blox Fruits disappear if the player moves too far away from them. This usually happens after about 30 seconds. Alternatively, the creatures also disappear automatically after 15 minutes if they have not been defeated by then.

♡

Roblox has collaborated with Gucci to host a digital storefront featuring limited-edition collectibles.

♡

Playtime is not counted in the AFK area of Royale High.

♡

All 14 horizontal sections in the Tower of Hell have German names.

Brain and heart in the right place

While millions of players worldwide express their creativity in the digital worlds he has created, the man behind the platform uses his influence to improve people's real lives. David Baszucki and his wife are deeply committed to charitable work. In March 2021, they established the Baszucki Brain Research Fund to support research into bipolar disorder. Their commitment continued in December of the same year with the Baszucki Lymphoma Therapeutics Initiative, which aims to improve the availability of therapies for lymphoma patients.

Wooden block with Christmas magic

The "Tió De Nadal" is a limited edition pet in Adopt Me! and has its origins in a Spanish Christmas fairy tale. The Tió de Nadal, also affectionately known as "Caga Tió," is a unique Christmas log figure and a popular tradition in Catalonia, Spain. It is a small log, often decorated with a friendly face, legs, and a red cap (a barretina).

Starting on December 8, the Tió is brought into the house and "fed" treats every day. On Christmas Day, the children sing a song and gently hit it with sticks while their parents secretly place candy or small gifts under its blanket. This is how the Tió "defecates" the gifts – a joyful tradition in Catalonia.

Haunting fun at Royale High

The "Blackwood Manor" realm was first introduced on October 23, 2021, as a temporary event for Royale High's Halloween event. Players had the opportunity to participate in a ghost hunting minigame where they could earn candy as a reward. The realm was originally removed on November 18, 2021, but returned for the Halloween events in 2022 (starting October 3) and 2023. One special feature concerned the equipment for ghost hunting: although players could equip the headlamp and night vision goggles as accessories in their character customization, these items were not permanently stored in the inventory. The only way to keep them for the future was to create a complete outfit while wearing the items.

Gentle words for tough leaps

Sometimes, the gaming world comes up with its own unique terms that make us smile. One of these is the renaming of the "Tower of Hell" to "Tower of Heck" on Roblox by younger players and some "child-friendly" YouTubers. They consider the word "hell" to be too crude or even a swear word, which is less of an issue for other players.

Death sounds good again

The famous "oof" sound that played in Roblox for years when an avatar died is a real classic for many players, almost as legendary as the game itself. The sound originally came from an old game by Tommy Tallarico and was later adopted by Roblox. But in 2022, the sound suddenly disappeared from the game due to licensing issues. For many in the community, this came as a bit of a shock: the iconic "oof" was gone, replaced by a generic sound that just didn't feel the same.

But in July 2025, there was a surprise: Roblox officially brought back the "oof" sound – accompanied by the announcement "comeback so good it hurts." The community reacted enthusiastically. Memes, reaction videos, and nostalgic comments flooded YouTube, TikTok, and Reddit. For many, it was a look back at their own childhood or the early days of their Roblox journey – a small sound with a big emotional impact.

Because let's be honest: no avatar death feels right unless it's accompanied by a dramatic "OOF!" Welcome back, you beautiful, painful sound.

One store, many questions

Fancy Furniture is a furniture store in the city of Bloxburg that does not offer any exclusive products. All items for sale there are identical to those available in the game's build mode. There is no official explanation as to why this store exists in the game when its entire inventory is available elsewhere.

Players have therefore come up with their own ideas about the purpose of the store. One popular theory is that the store is not yet finished and future updates may add exclusive items. Another hypothesis is that Fancy Furniture simply serves to make the game world more believable and encourage immersion in the game environment, without having any deeper purpose.

The turbo boost for your productivity

Have you ever wondered how successful people manage to maintain such high levels of productivity? When asked, David Baszucki revealed a remarkably straightforward strategy for preventing tasks from piling up: he deals with things as soon as they arise. For example, when an email arrives, he processes it immediately—he doesn't just read it and then put off deciding what to do next. This proven method saves valuable time, is highly efficient, and enables him to complete tasks immediately instead of postponing them.

Short and Sweet

The Stylez Hair Studio hair salon is located in Bloxburg. Occasionally, customers enter the salon and ask for a hairstyle or hair color that they already have.

♡

Mystery Box 1 was the first box in Murder Mystery 2 and was released with the Season 1 update.

♡

Thunderstorms in Grow a Garden occur at a frequency of approximately 2-3 seconds and can only be started by an administrator.

♡

"pathStraight" was the very first section designed for Tower of Hell. Although it was developed first, "Wall Wedges" was the section that actually made it into the game first.

From paintings, ghost drawers and... Bob

There are several hidden interactions in the DOORS lobby. Although there are no visible prompts, you can approach certain objects. A very quiet sound will indicate that you are in the right area.

The painting: To the left of the spawn point, you can interact with a painting. If you stand close enough to it, look at it, and press the "E" key, the title of the painting will appear on the screen – just like you remember from the hotel. Drawers in the backdoor area: At the end of the lobby interior, there are drawers that lead to the backdoor area.

Although you can't actually open them, pressing "E" triggers an interaction sound. At the same time, an error message appears in the console (F9). Bob (Trick or Treat Event): During the Trick or Treat Event, it was also possible to interact with Bob. If you looked at him closely and held down the "E" key, the text "... Nothing happens." appeared. This interaction worked the same way as in Jeff's store.

Animation tricks

In RIVLAS, there are two different reload animations for the spray, shotgun, revolver, and sniper weapons. The first is played during a regular reload. The second animation is used when the ammunition is completely empty and a full magazine is reloaded.

In contrast, the assault rifle, burst rifle, and pistol only have a single reload animation by default. However, there are certain skins that change this behavior: The Tommy Gun (assault rifle), FAMAS (burst rifle), and Hand Gun (pistol) have a special animation that only plays when the magazine is completely empty. This is a special feature of these skins, as the standard weapons do not have their own animation for this situation.

When Roblox Hits Pause

Sometimes in the real world, a public space must be closed to ensure the safety of the community before it can be reopened with new rules. A similar incident occurred in the digital world of Roblox. In February 2022, the popular "MeepCity" was suddenly closed temporarily after persistent criticism of its party feature. The platform responded to reports that this feature—originally intended for social gatherings—was increasingly being misused by older users for risky online dating encounters among the young player base. Although the game was only offline for a few hours, it returned with a permanent change: the source of the problem, the party feature, was permanently removed from the game.

Short and Sweet

The "Classic Squads" mode was the first game mode in BedWars, while "Classic Doubles" was introduced as the second mode.

♡

According to a developer, Timothy from the game DOORS has the best taste of all the characters.

♡

The hero and the sheriff cannot be active in the game at the same time. Only when the sheriff dies does an innocent person get the chance to pick up his weapon and become the hero himself.

♡

In Welcome to Bloxburg, you can significantly increase your income at work if all mood bars are at 81% or higher.

♡

The "Lamethrower" skin for the flamethrower in RIVALS is a tribute to the "Flamethrower" sold by The Boring Company.

From book to game

David Baszucki, the founder of Roblox, says he was inspired by Ernest Cline's books "Ready Player One" and "Ready Player Two." These books are about a huge, exciting digital world called OASIS. Imagine being able to live in a video game where you can do anything: go to school, go on adventures, and meet up with friends. That's exactly what OASIS is like! This idea, a huge online world that everyone can help shape and experience, helped David Baszucki develop Roblox. He wanted to create a similar platform where children and young people could build their own games and have fun together.

From the physics lab to the pixel world

Behind every great digital universe lies a lot of code and a groundbreaking idea. Sometimes, however, the origin of these ideas lies not in entertainment, but in practical application. Before co-creating the world of Roblox, David Baszucki developed the physics simulation software "Interactive Physics." This application allowed users to conduct and analyze mechanical and physical experiments virtually. It was this experience with the fundamental building blocks of interactive systems that brought the idea for Roblox to fruition and shifted the focus to a platform that allows users to design their own virtual worlds and games.

Short and Sweet

There is currently a run in DOORS that is considered the longest in the game. This route passes through a total of 1,250 doors – or, to be precise, 1,244. The journey begins at the rear entrance of the hotel, leads through the hotel and its rooms, and finally ends in the mines. Players pass through a total of 1,254 rooms, although the exact number is 1,248.

♡

MeepCity was originally called "Social-Meeps," a standalone project outside of Roblox from 2012. However, hardly anyone plays it anymore, and hardly anyone remembers it.

♡

"Home" is the 37th chapter in Piggy and was originally created for the April Fools' Day update for Piggy: Book 3. The chapter is unique in that it is the only one in the entire Piggy series in which there are no enemies and players cannot die.

The hunt for the giant tomato

"You have to sow to reap," as the saying goes. If you really want to make it big in the Roblox experience "Grow a Garden", you sometimes have to come up with something extraordinary. This is especially true for anyone who wants to unlock the rare "Giant Tomato" achievement. To get this achievement, it's not enough to harvest an average tomato. No, you have to sell a tomato that weighs at least 7 kg and is a real showpiece! To achieve this goal, you should invest in a variety of non-limited sprinklers, such as Grandmaster Sprinklers, Master Sprinklers, Godly Sprinklers, Advanced Sprinklers, or Basic Sprinklers.

How ideas quickly become reality

The Roblox platform is home to hundreds of talented developers who are constantly creating new and impressive worlds. What many people don't know is that sometimes it doesn't take long for an idea to become a finished game. A prime example is the popular shooter RIVALS from "Nosniy Games." The game, released by the developer community around "Nosniy" and "SenseiWarrior" on June 28, 2024, had an astonishingly short main development time of only five to six months.

Short and Sweet

All pets in Grow a Garden that are no longer available are technically still available. This is possible by giving away or saving older eggs, as these contain the rare pets.

♡

In Welcome to Bloxburg, there is a small, remote island that can be discovered in the vast ocean. If you swim there, you will find a volleyball that is unusually covered in grass. This is probably a reference to Wilson, the famous volleyball from the movie "Cast Away."

♡

Buying every permanent fruit in Blox Fruits would cost $68,055, while buying every fruit from the Blox Fruit Dealer would cost $83,582,500.

MeepCity in XXL mode

Sometimes it's not just the Meeps that grow in Meep-City – in 2019, a few players really made it big! Literally, because they used special scripts to make their characters huge in the game. The cool thing was that these gigantic avatars were visible to everyone, not just on their own screens. This was made possible by a vulnerability in the Roblox avatar system that allowed normally locked settings to be changed. A Reddit user summed it up at the time: "It's a script that uses the system to increase the size of the characters." Many found it exciting to walk around MeepCity as giants and tried the trick for as long as it worked.

Roblox's frontrunner

With a staggering number of over 46.6 billion visits (as of April 25, 2024), Brookhaven RP has established itself as by far the most popular game in the vast Roblox world. This virtual phenomenon offers players the opportunity to live in a vibrant city, own impressive houses, drive stylish vehicles, and experience a variety of exciting adventures. Although Brookhaven RP is the clear number one, there are other Roblox games that also have a considerable fan base. "Adopt Me!" and "Blox Fruits" are two such titles, boasting impressive numbers with 36 billion and 32.8 billion visits, respectively.

Wordplay or currency?

You know Robux as the virtual currency used on the Roblox platform, but do you know where the name of this currency comes from? The name "Robux" was coined by Roblox employee John Shedletsky and is a play on words combining 'ROBLOX' and "BUX" (bucks).

Traces that remain forever

February 11, 2013, was a sad day for the Roblox community, as the Roblox team announced via its Twitter account that Erik Cassel had lost his battle with cancer at the age of 45. Erik was a co-founder, administrator, and former vice president of engineering at Roblox. As a sign of mourning, hundreds of users gathered the very next day, February 12, 2013, at a specially created memorial site, the Erik Cassel Memorial. Many of them dressed like Erik's game character to pay their last respects. Roblox also honored Cassel in other ways: On February 15, 2013, a classic shirt titled "Official Erik Shirt" was released in his memory. However, this special garment was only available for eight days. Another gesture of remembrance was the renaming of the "Well-Worn Hat" to "Erik Cassel's Hut," which was also available for purchase for a short period of time.

Bed dismantling gone wrong

The bed is at the center of BedWars. A well-known glitch in the game is that a bed is not destroyed, but instead turns black. This occurs when a player attempts to dismantle the bed with a tool, but then quickly switches to another tool. Normally, the progress of dismantling a bed is recorded continuously. However, with the aforementioned glitch, the player's client transmits incorrect progress data to the server, for example, "Progress: 100 -> 80 -> 95 -> 60." In this case, the server blocks all further attempts to dismantle the bed as soon as it has recorded a progress of 80. To work around this problem, it was previously necessary for another player to help with the dismantling. Since their progress was not blocked, they were able to successfully destroy the bed. The bug has now been largely fixed. A black bed can now be destroyed after another attempt at dismantling.

Player or godparent?

What do an archaeologist naming an ancient statue and a Roblox player in a horror game have in common? More than you might think. It has been revealed that the terrifying creatures in DOORS didn't originally have official names. The names we know today, which are considered canonical in the gaming world, were given by the character you control. So you gave them their names.

DOORS songs in legal limbo

In early September 2022, a case of copyright infringement on Spotify involving Roblox caused a stir. A user had published the soundtrack of the game DOORS on the platform without permission. The problem was that the user claimed copyright for the songs. He reported all users who had used the music for copyright infringement, even though he himself was not the legal owner of the rights. However, the situation was later clarified and the infringement was rectified.

Little ship, big impact

The Sloop is the most effective ship in Blox Fruits for players participating in naval events in the Second Sea as part of the navy. Its advantage lies in the fact that it has the same high number of hit points as larger boats, but is significantly less expensive. Due to its compact size, the Sloop has another advantage: it makes it easier to appear as a large ship during ship raids and to evade attacks from sea beasts more easily. However, there are also disadvantages. These include its slow turning speed and the impractical placement of the shipwright mini-game, which is located in close proximity to the cannon seat and the driver's seat.

The dummy shows no mercy

The training dummy, a level 1500 opponent, is waiting for you behind the arena trainer. Its attacks have zero delay and it is immediately knocked back, making it impossible to use certain combos. For example, you cannot use combinations such as "Godhuman [C] followed by Kitsune [F] or Gas [Z]". After Godhuman [C], the dummy is immediately thrown so far away that the subsequent attack misses. This also happens with other combos, such as "Phoenix C followed by Phoenix M1" or "Godhuman [C] followed by Quake [Z]". This effect occurs because opponents are directly connected to the server and therefore have virtually zero ping.

DynaBlocks was yesterday, Roblox is today

In the world of technology, there are many stories of successful projects that started out with a different name or as a prototype. It's like a caterpillar turning into a butterfly. The development of Roblox followed a similar path. Long before the game became the platform that connects millions of people worldwide, David Baszucki and Erik Cassel started developing it in 2003 under the name "DynaBlocks." It was only after being renamed Roblox in 2005 and released for Windows and macOS that it was finally made available to the general public by Roblox Corporation in 2006.

Clean in record time

Who would have thought that cleaning up could be so much fun? In the "Cleaning Simulator" experience, you take on the role of a superstar janitor who keeps things tidy with a mop and spray bottle. A remarkable record in the history of the game is the speedrun by "videm" (USA) on July 20, 2017. He completed a solo run without activated moon gravity in just 22 minutes and 45.96 seconds, a result that has been verified by Speedrun. Maybe you should invite him over for your next big cleaning session.

Generative AI Hits Roblox

The rapid development of artificial intelligence is shaping our world in more and more ways, from science to art. It is also leaving its mark on the world of Roblox and virtual experiences: In spring 2024, Roblox Studio introduced two innovative generative AI tools designed to significantly speed up and simplify the content creation workflow. These smart features include automatic avatar customization, which allows developers to transform raw data from 3D body meshes into vivid, fully animated avatars in a flash, and textile generation, which uses a text-to-image model to generate realistic textures based on simple text descriptions.

There are currently around 150 different maps in Bedwars.

One Piece Adventure in Roblox

Are you a big fan of One Piece? Then Blox Fruits is exactly the adventure you should experience. This action-adventure game on Roblox takes you into a huge world that is heavily inspired by the popular anime series. In Blox Fruits, you take on the role of a brave pirate or a valiant naval officer and discover powerful abilities that you gain through special fruits. Each of these "Blox fruits" gives you unique abilities – from flying attacks to devastating fireballs or gigantic transformations.

The game constantly challenges you to exciting battles against enemies and other players, allowing you to gain experience to improve your skills and become stronger. At the same time, you can customize your character by investing in various attributes such as melee combat or defense. On your journey, you explore numerous islands, travel with your ship, and face fearsome bosses while discovering hidden treasures and exciting quests.

By the way, did you know that "Blox Fruits" was originally called "Blox Piece"? To avoid legal issues with the creators of One Piece, the name was changed – as were some of the fruits that had to be adapted in the game.

Size, color, speed

In Piggy, there are often significant differences between the bot characters that players encounter and the skins of the same name that they can use themselves. These differences include unique animations, different speeds, special abilities, and varying visual and acoustic details. Some bots exhibit individual behaviors: Piggy, Mother, Father, Sheepy, Teacher, Grandmother, Frostiggy, and The Prototype, for example, have their own animations for running, idling, and jump scares. Willow's bot in the factory also uses a special idle animation. Grandmother and Gryffyn's bots move slower than the standard speed of other Piggy bots. Certain bots have special attacks or mechanics: Mr. P and Willow can stun players by shooting at them. The bots Markus, Piggy (Distorted), and Ombra can teleport. The ??? bot uses a unique running animation before it spots a player and is just as fast as the survivors. Blatt's bot is silent and only chases players when the Scry bot has spotted them. Eelektra can be distracted, but becomes more aggressive afterwards. The Duocara bot changes its face after a certain amount of time, making it faster. With the skin, this change is purely cosmetic and has no effect on speed. The appearance and sounds can also vary. Unlike their skins, the Rash, Tigry, Willow, and Poley bots are not infected. Poley also has a larger hat, different animations, and a different weapon. The Sentinel bots have a fixed color, while their skin changes color. Gryffyn as a bot uses 2022 textures and does not change color after a kill, while the skin with 2020 textures does.

Short and Sweet

Previously, the "bomb" item could destroy sections in Tower of Hell, allowing players to make sections impassable; however, this has been fixed.

♡

"Anticipation" and "Blank" are extremely rare sections in the game. Their spawn chance is a negligible 0.000067563%. This makes them the rarest sections in the entire game. In addition, Anticipation has the special feature of only being able to appear at the bottom of a tower.

♡

When you jump into the air using a jump or gravity coil, the jumps in the air make the same sound as jumps on the ground.

♡

The finish section in Tower of Hell is the only section that extends beyond the normal width of the tower.

From the iris to the heart of the infection

The eye color of infected individuals in Piggy, often referred to as pupil colors, can provide information about what the creature was like before infection. Currently, eight different pupil colors are recognized: red, orange, yellow, green, blue, purple, white, and black. In addition, there are six recognized colors for the sclera (the white part of the eye): black, white, red, blue, green, and gold. Examples of pupil colors and their meanings:

Orange: Although little is known about this type, they are known to be able to move long distances almost instantly and often travel in groups.

Yellow: These infected individuals helped their community before they became infected.

Green: People with green pupils were very independent before infection.

Black (with orange iris): This type of infected person has a connection to the so-called "Insolence." Like those infected with orange pupils, they can also move almost instantly over long distances and often travel in groups.

Most Roblox players use a cell phone or tablet: around 80% log in this way. Around 17% mainly play on a computer, and only 3% use a game console such as Xbox or PlayStation.

Short and Sweet

The entity "Guiding Light" acts as the player's grim reaper on the main floors. On the side floors, however, this role is taken over by the entity "Curious Light." Although Curious Light is also present on all main floors, it does not appear to the player in the role of grim reaper there.

♡

Approximately 21 percent of Roblox players live in the US and Canada. Around 26 percent come from Europe.

The rest is spread across the eastern Pacific region (25 percent) and other parts of the world (28 percent).

♡

Although the fruit "Buddha" in Blox Fruits is named after the famous figure from Buddhism, the icon is actually Budai. This Chinese monk, also known as the "laughing monk," is often mistakenly regarded as the Buddha.

Door handles that buy dreams

In real life, we encounter countless things that seem worthless until someone decides to assign value to them. Just like an old stamp or a simple stone that suddenly becomes a work of art, an ordinary everyday object can become a symbol of "wealth" in another world. This is also the case in the in-game world of "DOORS" on Roblox, where simple door handles, known as knobs, are not only used to open doors, but are also traded as the game's primary currency.

But for the true patrons, those who have already invested at least 2,400 Robux in their adventure, a very special door opens: a secret area in the shop is revealed, offering three exclusive packages of knobs to reward those players who have already proven their willingness to make significant investments. The purchase options are: 6,000 Knobs for 999 Robux, 16,000 Knobs for 2,499 Robux, 1,000,000 Knobs for 100,000 Robux.

Bloxburg is leaving permanent construction mode

Welcome to Bloxburg was frequently criticized for being permanently in beta status. For a whopping eight years. When you first logged in as a player, you were greeted with a message stating that the game was still in beta and that errors could occur. You had to click away this message before you could see the actual menu. Since Welcome to Bloxburg became free to play on June 15, 2024, this message has been removed. The paragraph asking players to send suggestions or bug reports to the developer Coeptus via their Twitter account is also no longer part of the game.

From drops to dream melons

Wondering how to get the most out of your moonmelons in Grow a Garden? Then you should try the sprinkler method. This effective strategy simply requires you to place sprinklers around your crop and leave the game unattended for at least 30 minutes. After the appropriate mutations, moonmelons grow to an impressive size, driving their selling price up to rival that of sugar blossoms.

Blue Skirt, Big Mystery

Have you encountered the "Ghost of Brookhaven" yet? It is described as a doll with a blue skirt, long black hair, and an eerie face, and is the subject of much speculation. Contrary to the widespread belief among many players that it is the daughter of Mr. and Mrs. Brookhaven, this is not correct. Mr. and Mrs. Brookhaven are known to have had only one son named Marcus.

Roblox + Sims = Bloxburg happiness

Welcome to Bloxburg is a simulation and role-playing game originally developed by Coeptus. However, the game has since changed hands and is now owned by Coffee Stain Studios, which continues to develop it under the name Bloxburg Development. The name of the game is a combination of "Roblox" and 'Simburg' – a reference to the well-known game series "The Sims."

As the name suggests, it is a life simulation game based on the Roblox platform. In the virtual world of Bloxburg, you can design your own life and build your dream home. The gameplay is very similar to the popular "The Sims" series: it offers the opportunity to build and lead a virtual existence.

The boomerang among waste bins

In the experience "The Strongest Battlegrounds", the ability to throw trash cans is subject to a special rule regarding death counters. If a thrown trash can hits a player with an active death counter, that counter returns and strikes the original thrower of the trash can. This is a significant change from previous versions of the game. At the beginning of The Strongest Battlegrounds, bypassing the death counter was one of the biggest advantages of the trash can. However, the update removed this tactic and made the trash can equal to other attacks in terms of the death counter mechanism.

Charming spelling mistakes

"Criss Cross Applesauce" is known as the comfortable cross-legged position that children often adopt in preschool or elementary school to stay calm and attentive. But did you know that this term also has a funny little story in Tower of Hell? There are two sections in the game called "Criss Cross" and "Apple Suace." Yep, there's a spelling mistake in the second section – it should actually be "Apple Sauce." The developer thought the mistake was so funny that he left it in the game.

Short and Sweet

On January 3, 2024, SizzleBurger, one of the largest restaurant role-playing games on Roblox, celebrated its 10th anniversary! Founded in 2014 by SilverAuthority, the community continues to serve virtual burgers with team spirit and fun every day.

♡

In the world of BedWars, there is speculation that there may be a romantic relationship between the Spirit Catcher and Gompy. This assumption is based on various emotes in the game that hint at such a connection.

♡

Many members of The Strongest Battlegrounds community find the character Deadly Ninja very unpopular. The main reason for this is that he makes it very easy for players to run away, steal kills, and spam attacks continuously.

Hide and distract with style

Emotes in Murder Mystery 2 do not offer any direct gameplay advantages, but can be both risky and useful for innocent players. Items such as the "firefly jar" or the "prank bomb" may reveal your position. Even pulling out some emote items can be misunderstood by sheriffs. On the other hand, emotes such as "Sitting" allow for better hiding places, and a well-timed "prank bomb" can distract the killer, allowing you to escape. There were also glitches that allowed the simultaneous use of "Teddy Bear" and knives or the penetration of walls, the latter of which has since been fixed.

When sprinting makes everything bigger

When you sprint in the Experience "Piggy", the screen zooms out slightly. If you successfully escape while your character is sprinting, the zoomed-out view will remain in the main menu and during the following cutscene. However, this "issue" can be easily fixed by clicking "play." Previously, this zoom effect remained for the entire duration of a game session. Fortunately, this bug was fixed at a later date.

Short and Sweet

The Star Scepter from Royale High is an accessory inspired by Star Guardian Lux's staff from the game League of Legends.

♡

Users spend an average of $15 per month on Robux.

♡

Since China has certain laws governing video games, the game mode "Infection" has been renamed "Turn" in the Chinese version of Piggy.

♡

There are currently 146 NPCs in Blox Fruits, some of which were inspired by developers and well-known YouTubers.

♡

Robux, the virtual currency on Roblox, basically refers to a variety of game tokens, while the singular is called „Robuk".

Short and Sweet

Compared to other weapons in RIVALS, the Exogun has the fastest reload time.

♡

Unlike Sam, who was replaced by Tom, the shopkeeper NPC Steven remained in Grow a Garden and was only fixed when necessary.

♡

With the Yeti Kit, you can increase the damage of the axe in BedWars.

♡

Jeff and El Goblino are considered best friends in the world of DOORS.

♡

Originally, the character "Sally" was referred to as "Window" by the DOORS community. This nickname came about because she always appeared in the same place, near a window. It was only later that her official name became known.

The fountain of youth for giant birds

Some say that wisdom comes with age. And in many areas of nature, that's true. But in the world of Roblox, or more specifically in the "Grow a Garden" experience, there is a curious exception to this rule. There, the valuable breeding bonus that an ostrich gains with age reaches its maximum value at 10. From this point on, neither its weight nor its age play any further role in increasing its abilities.

For this reason, it is not recommended to invest time and effort in further training an ostrich or hatching a particularly large specimen that exceeds this point, as this will not bring any additional benefits. However, that's not the end of the story!

You can increase the total bonus by using several ostriches at the same time, thereby increasing the pet's age beyond 10. In this way, it is possible to hatch an animal up to level 80 immediately by using, for example, eight ostriches with the maximum age bonus of 10 each at the same time.

Short and Sweet

If the murderer and the sheriff (or hero) are shot at the same time in Murder Mystery 2, the game displays the results, but both player symbols are marked with an X – a sign that they have been eliminated. Nevertheless, the sheriff is declared the winner.

♡

The player "DerHausaufgabe" has the most sequel sections within the main game Tower of Hell with 7 sections (Death Jump, Dices, Dropping, Faster Movement, The Agents Deja Vu, The Agents Escape, and The Phantoms Return).

♡

Before the character descriptions were removed, the description of the Destructive Cyborg in The Strongest Battlegrounds was: "He will turn you into modern art."

Lava Freeze Trick Explained

The Dungeon is a subrealm in Campus 3 in the Roblox experience "Royale High," which is unlocked via a puzzle in the Throne Tower. Once this puzzle is solved, not only is access to the Dungeon granted, but a teleport option is also activated in the Teleport Scepter.

To find your way around the Dungeon, it is important to follow the rules.Any attempt to move outside the designated map will result in the player being reset immediately. This also applies to Cell 3: it can only be entered through its door, as glitches do not work here. It is also not possible to look into the cell with the crystal ball. Even if you manage to get into Cell 3 through a glitch, the chest inside cannot be opened.

An important tool for players is a translation sheet hidden on the back of the Nature Throne at the end of the Obbys. This sheet helps to decipher the language that appears in the cutscene. There is a useful trick for the obby section: after the door from the element room has been opened, but before the lava rises, all items should be dropped. Then position yourself directly at the door and stay there until the lava has completely stopped rising. Once the screen returns to its normal color, you have unlimited time for the obby.

Freezing until the door opens

“The Vault” is a secret section within Tower of Hell developed by uwuPyxl, distinguished by its unique ice doors that set it apart from the rest of the game. The doors are made almost entirely of ice, with only the keypad, handle, and dark gray brackets as details, giving them a smooth, plastic-like texture. Entering the correct access codes triggers a green “CORRECT” display and opens the doors, while troll codes show a red “NAH” with empty contents, and entering the number “69” produces a red “NICE” Easter egg.

The Inverted Monkey Mystery

The Silver Monkey, a legendary pet, was introduced with the Animal Update. The chance of obtaining it is 42.55% by hatching the Legendary Egg. There are some notable features regarding this pet's mutations. If the Silver Monkey has the Inverted mutation and is placed in a player's garden, only its eye color will change. The rest of the model remains unchanged. This is most likely a bug, as the pet icon for the Inverted Silver Monkey shows the entire model with inverted colors. A similar behavior can be seen with the Golden mutation: The Silver Monkey simply emits golden rays of light instead of turning completely gold.

Greek heroine or special forces?

A name that sounds like a battle cry, but sounds like a letter: It sounds like an ancient Greek heroine, but the name Delta, which you probably already know from the experience "Piggy: Book 2", has a much harsher meaning. Although the name Delta is often used as a female first name of Greek origin, referring to the fourth letter of the Greek alphabet, it is unclear whether this has any connection to the character's gender. It is more likely that the name derives from its military meaning. In a military context, "Delta" often refers to a special unit (for example, a unit of the U.S. Army) responsible for counterterrorism and hostage rescue. This assumption is supported by the setting of the chapter "Camp," which has a military connection.

Leaderboard Madness

The rankings in Murder Mystery 2 are based on a dynamic collection of player data and statistics, generated from the most recent rankings and largely sourced from the Murder Mystery 2 Leaderboard Discord Server archive. About half an hour before the end of a ranking period, players sometimes report unexpected point gains of 1,000 to 3,000, often caused by last-minute data synchronization. These spikes typically result from intensive "grinding," sometimes using second accounts or private servers, to boost scores shortly before the period ends.

From zero to gold in one match

The ranked mode in BedWars, often referred to simply as Ranked, was introduced with the update on November 5, 2021. It allows you to compete against other players in a competitive system and work your way up a leaderboard. Players who meet the requirements for this mode but have not yet achieved a rank in a given season will be assigned the Bronze rank.

It is interesting to observe how the ranks can develop: a single victory in a Ranked match can promote a player to the Gold+ rank, while three victories may only be enough for the Silver rank. These correlations have been confirmed in a video by the YouTuber "MiniBloxia", among others.

The sixth season of Ranked mode stands out in particular as it was the longest of all seasons at 127 days. Another noteworthy detail is that even for second place in a Ranked Squad game, players received at least one RP (Ranked Point) as long as they survived for at least ten minutes.

There used to be more than there is today

Sometimes it feels as though things change over time and lose some of their original charm. This also applies to the world of video games: "Legacy Adopt Me!", the original paid version of the popular "Adopt Me!" game, offered a remarkable server capacity of up to 200 players at a time, compared to just 48 players in the current version. In addition, this earlier version focused exclusively on adopting babies, long before pets became the hallmark of Adopt Me!

Floating secrets

The Underwater City is one of seven islands that house a portal. The others are: Castle on the Sea, Hydra Island, Kingdom of Rose, Cursed Ship, Skylands/Upper Skylands, and Floating Turtle. What sets the Underwater City apart from the others is its unique portal system, which is completely different from the models used on the other islands. The island gets its name because it is the only one that is supposedly underwater. Although the city is depicted as an "underwater metropolis," players can see a round, dome-shaped island on the horizon outside the main area. The invisible barrier surrounding the island has a gap near the fishing commandos. Those who find it can circle the dome and even swim through the dome's shell, as it does not collide with the player.

From the catwalk to chaos

You've gotten all dressed up for a party and realize at the last minute that your hairstyle is perfect, but your shoes suddenly look like they came out of a cartoon. In Royale High, where you as the player have control over your appearance, a similar but funny problem can arise.

The game lets you customize your character with countless details, from body types to role-playing names and diaries. The selection of clothes, hairstyles, skirts, heels, faces, wings, and mermaid tails is huge. Sometimes, combining all these things can lead to a small glitch.

For example, if you recolor a skirt, the heels may be displayed incorrectly. To fix this, simply remove the heels and put them back on again. A similar problem can occur with mermaid fins, where either the legs show through or the fins move uncontrollably even though you are not in the water. Again, removing the fins and then reattaching them will fix the error.

Short and Sweet

The sections "Red Cylinders of Doom," "Legos Struction Site," and "Points of the Compass" are the vanilla sections with the longest names if you ignore the spaces. However, if you count the spaces, only "Red Cylinders of Doom" and "Points of the Compass" share the title of longest name.

♡

There are currently 34 bosses in Blox Fruits. Most of them have a spawn time of 20 to 45 minutes, with raid bosses being an exception (as of July 2025).

♡

In Blox Fruits, Longma not only has the lowest amount of health points of all the bosses in the Third Sea, but also has an interesting name history. Longma is named after a winged horse with dragon scales from Chinese mythology "Long" means "dragon" and "Mǎ" means "horse".

Short and Sweet

When you use the "Camouflage" ability in Piggy, you lose the ability to operate doors, whether to open or close them. Interestingly, this restriction does not apply to the build mode.

The beanstalkvine from Grow a Garden is inspired by the fairy tale "Jack and the Beanstalk."

In the "Pride TV" section of Tower of Hell, there is a little something special hidden behind the television: "BlackyBounty-Browny TM." This is a direct tribute from DerHausaufgabe to his three pet rats named Blacky, Bounty, and Browny.

In Brookhaven RP, there's no way around the club. It's the most popular place in the entire game.

Regenerating Rage

You're the shining hero of a popular game and looking for an easy challenge. A training dummy seems like the perfect opportunity to practice a few punches. But then comes the big disappointment: this dummy is tougher than you thought.

The NPC "Weakest Dummy" in The Strongest Battlegrounds has the same amount of health as you, the player: 100 HP. Until now, many thought he was an easy opponent because he didn't regenerate. But that's a thing of the past: since May 2024, the dummy regenerates all its health instantly if it isn't attacked for 10 to 20 seconds.

Collectibles for true fans

For anyone who enjoys cool gaming collectibles, there's an exciting trick. The unique weapons "Dartbringer" and "SharkSeeker" in Murder Mystery 2 could only be obtained by participating in a collaboration with Nerf. You had to buy real Nerf blasters, which contained a promotional code that unlocked the weapons in the game. To this day, these are the only weapons that can be obtained in this way.

Glitches that reinvent knives

The “Knifeception” effect is an enhancement for the knife in Murder Mystery 2, which you can purchase for 300 diamonds in the shop. Although this effect is visually appealing, there are several known bugs that affect its appearance. A notable bug occurs when the Knifeception effect is equipped with the “Virtual” knife, as it emits a green blade instead of the expected blue. A similar issue occurs when the “Eternal” knife is used, with ‘Seers’ displayed as projected knives instead of “Eternals.” Furthermore, a glitch affects all vintage knives: when equipped with the Knifeception effect, the corresponding vintage blade does not appear and is replaced by the original Classic Knife, the default knife provided to players at the beginning of Murder Mystery 2.

Luxury, But Low Ceiling

The real estate industry is often about exclusivity and special features. And just like in the real world, such details can also be found in the fictional universes of online games. One example of this is the Luxury Apartments in Adopt Me! in Roblox. This impressive building spans six floors and boasts 22 rooms. What makes these apartments special is a feature they share with the Millionaire's Villa: the explicit designation of parking spaces. While the Millionaire's Villa only has one parking space, the Luxury Apartments stand out with twice that number – namely two parking spaces. However, these are not easy to use due to their low height.

Short and Sweet

Once you reach level 50 in a job in Welcome to Bloxburg, you will receive a special reward: the Excellence Award. To reach this level, the "Excellent Employee" game pass is almost essential. Without it, most players will find it very difficult to meet the necessary requirements.

♡

In BedWars, obsidian is a building block that plays a special role. It is the most expensive building material in the game and can be purchased for one emerald per four blocks. It is important to note that obsidian cannot be purchased individually, but only in packs of four blocks.

♡

Rumor has it that the green man in Brookhaven RP's hospital is the corpse of Mr. Brookhaven.

Your virtual life awaits

Brookhaven RP is currently the most visited experience on Roblox, and if you've been playing for a while, you've probably already visited it. This captivating game was created by Roblox game developer "Wolfpaq" in collaboration with "Aidanleewolf."

In Brookhaven RP, you'll dive into a dynamic world where you can not only explore the expansive map, but also acquire a variety of vehicles and items. These items are not just for fun, but also support your role-playing and make it easier to navigate the lively environment.

A special feature of Brookhaven RP are the unique houses available to you. You can customize these houses, choosing from a diverse selection of house types to create your perfect virtual home. Each house has a safe, but it serves more of a decorative function, as it only contains cash that can be "looted" by other players.

Brookhaven RP also offers you extensive avatar customization options. You can choose from a wide range of items based on your personal preferences and even change your name to personalize your virtual identity. You probably already knew all of this, but did you also know that the name of the experience is based on the real city of Brookhaven in the US state of Georgia?

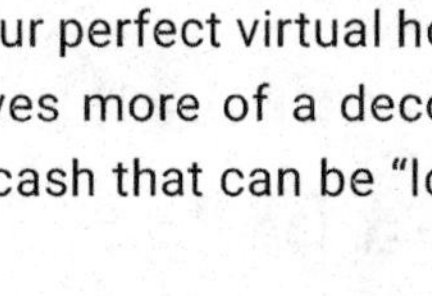

In the 2019 Easter event, there were 11 hidden eggs to find, and if you collected them all, you received a trophy and a badge as a reward.

Epilogue

Congratulations, adventurer! You have completed an exciting journey through the colorful world of Roblox. In this book, you have discovered treasures—amazing facts and little secrets that would surprise even experienced players.

Sometimes it's the little things that make a game special: the stories behind the characters, the unusual locations, or the fun surprises the game has in store for you.

And even if this knowledge may not directly help you master a difficult game level, it's still fun to show off, right? Put your friends to the test and impress them with your newly acquired Roblox knowledge.

Whether you're a pro at creating games or just starting to design your world, stay curious! There's always something new to discover, both in Roblox and in the world around you. So grab your gear and get ready—adventure awaits!

Imprint

We used Textstudio.com to generate parts of the cover texts.

https://www.textstudio.com/

Some of the icons used in this book have been provided courtesy of Streamline.

https://www.streamlinehq.com/icons

1. Edition

Johannes Schwegler und Oliver Hagel GbR
c/o Block Services
Stuttgarter Str. 106
70736 Fellbach
Deutschland

Printed in Dunstable, United Kingdom

76232738R00077